My SPANISH
Sticker Dictionary

el sol
el sol

el avión
el abee-<u>on</u>

el león
el leh-<u>on</u>

hello
buenos días
<u>bway</u>-noss <u>dee</u>-ass

written by Catherine Bruzzone & Vicky Barker

illustrated by Vicky Barker

Spanish advisor: Rosi Perea

 sourcebooks
eXplore

Text and illustrations copyright © 2022 by b small publishing • This edition © 2022 by Sourcebooks
Sourcebooks and the colophon are registered trademarks of Sourcebooks. • All rights reserved.
Digital technology was used to prepare the full color art. • Published by Sourcebooks eXplore an imprint of Sourcebooks Kids
P.O. Box 4410, Naperville, Illinois 60567–4410 • (630) 961-3900 • sourcebookskids.com
Cataloging-in-Publication Data is on file with the Library of Congress. • Source of Production: China
Date of Production: August 2022 • Run Number: 5027142 • Printed and bound in China. • WKT 10 9 8 7 6 5 4 3 2 1

Las palabras útiles - Useful words

lass pa-<u>lab</u>-rass <u>oot</u>-ee-less

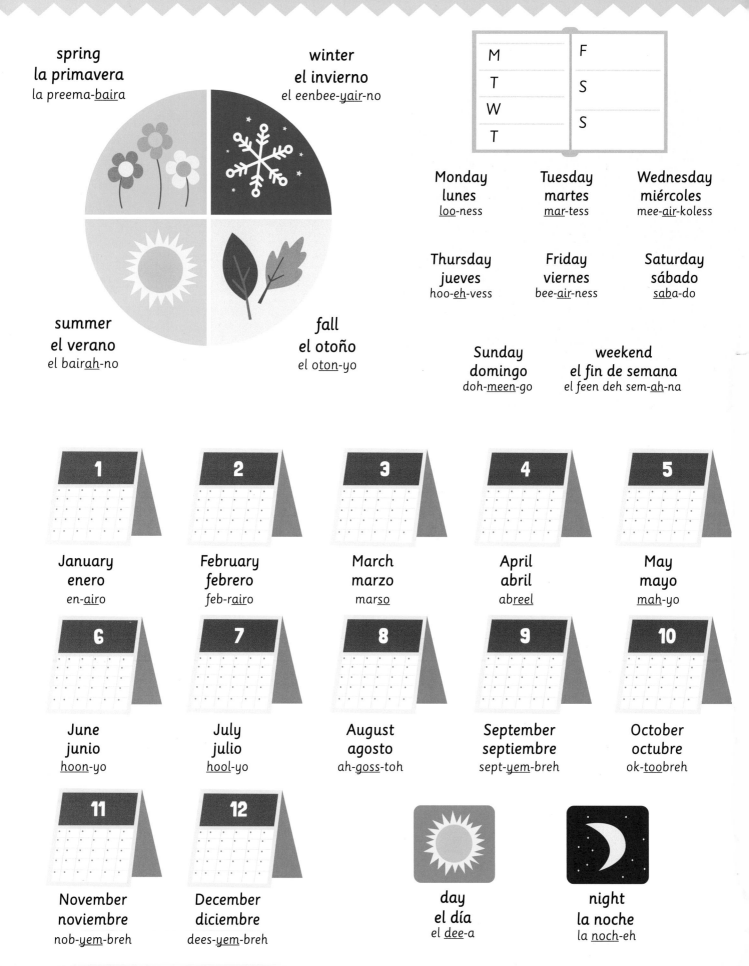

spring
la primavera
la preema-<u>baira</u>

winter
el invierno
el eenbee-<u>yair</u>-no

summer
el verano
el bair<u>ah</u>-no

fall
el otoño
el o<u>ton</u>-yo

M	F
T	S
W	S
T	

Monday
lunes
<u>loo</u>-ness

Tuesday
martes
<u>mar</u>-tess

Wednesday
miércoles
mee-<u>air</u>-koless

Thursday
jueves
hoo-<u>eh</u>-vess

Friday
viernes
bee-<u>air</u>-ness

Saturday
sábado
<u>saba</u>-do

Sunday
domingo
doh-<u>meen</u>-go

weekend
el fin de semana
el feen deh sem-<u>ah</u>-na

January
enero
en-<u>airo</u>

February
febrero
feb-r<u>airo</u>

March
marzo
mar<u>so</u>

April
abril
ab<u>reel</u>

May
mayo
<u>mah</u>-yo

June
junio
<u>hoon</u>-yo

July
julio
<u>hool</u>-yo

August
agosto
ah-<u>goss</u>-toh

September
septiembre
sept-<u>yem</u>-breh

October
octubre
ok-<u>too</u>breh

November
noviembre
nob-<u>yem</u>-breh

December
diciembre
dees-<u>yem</u>-breh

day
el día
el <u>dee</u>-a

night
la noche
la <u>noch</u>-eh

Índice - Contents
een-dee-seh

You'll find the stickers in the middle of the book!

please
por favor
pohr fab-or

thank you
gracias
gras-ee-ass

yes
sí
see

no
no
noh

left
la izquierda
la eez-kier-da

right
la derecha
la der-eh-cha

En la granja
en la gran-ha

cow

el gato
el gat-o

horse

el gallo
el gah-yo

hen

What noise does a cow make?

On the farm

el perro
el <u>pehr</u>-ro

sheep

goat

pig

duck

Put a "¡bravo!" sticker here when you complete the page.

Los medios de transporte

loss <u>meh</u>-dee-ohss de transport-eh

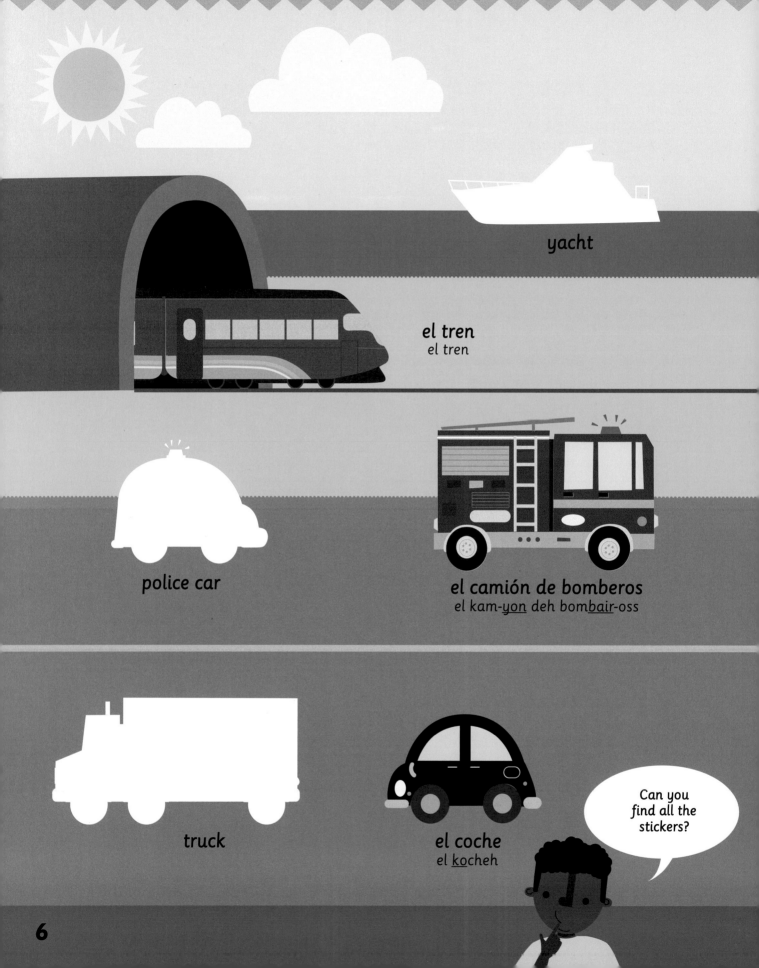

yacht

el tren
el tren

police car

el camión de bomberos
el kam-<u>yon</u> deh bom<u>bair</u>-oss

truck

el coche
el <u>kocheh</u>

Can you find all the stickers?

Transportation

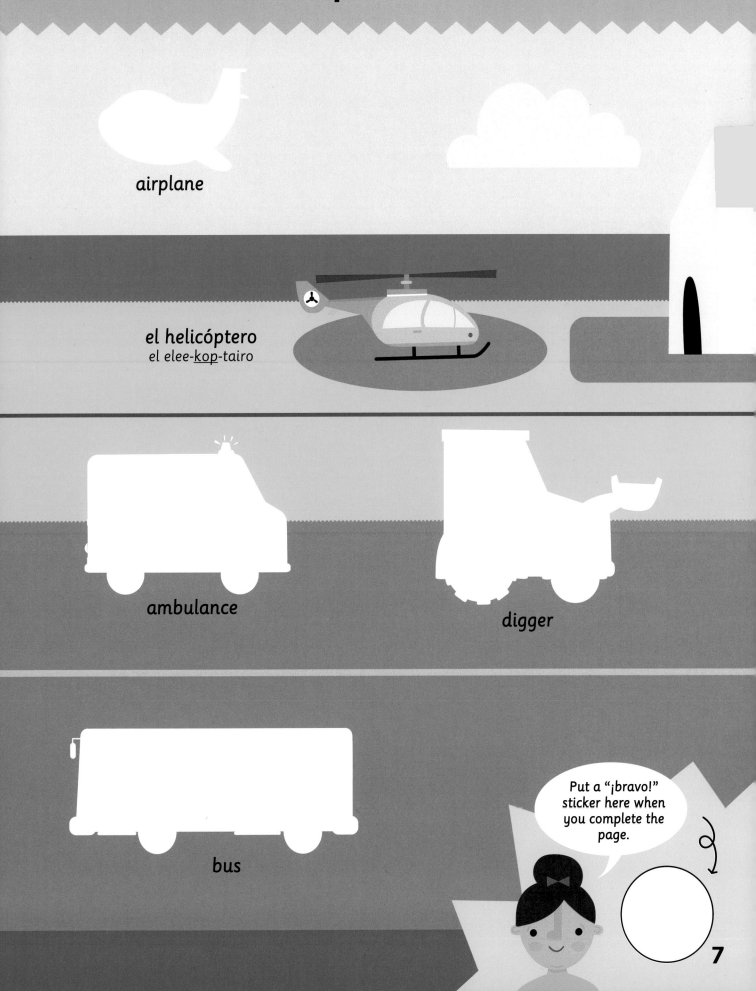

airplane

el helicóptero
el elee-<u>kop</u>-tairo

ambulance

digger

bus

Put a "¡bravo!" sticker here when you complete the page.

7

En el zoológico
en el soh-<u>loh</u>-hee-koh

lion

el hipopótamo
el eepo-<u>pot</u>-tam-o

el elefante
el eleh-<u>fan</u>-teh

crocodile

What is your
favorite
animal?

At the zoo

monkey

giraffe

polar bear

zebra

tiger

Put a "¡bravo!" sticker here when you complete the page.

9

En la playa
en la pl<u>ah</u>-ya

sailboat

el mar
el mar

el / la surfista
el/la soor-<u>fee</u>sta

crab

seagull

Can you walk
like a crab?

At the beach

la arena
la ah-<u>reh</u>na

la sombrilla
la som<u>bree</u>-ya

beach chair

shell

el castillo de arena
el kas<u>tee</u>-yo deh ah-<u>reh</u>na

pail

starfish

Put a "¡bravo!" sticker here when you complete the page.

Los números
loss noo-mair-oss

Numbers

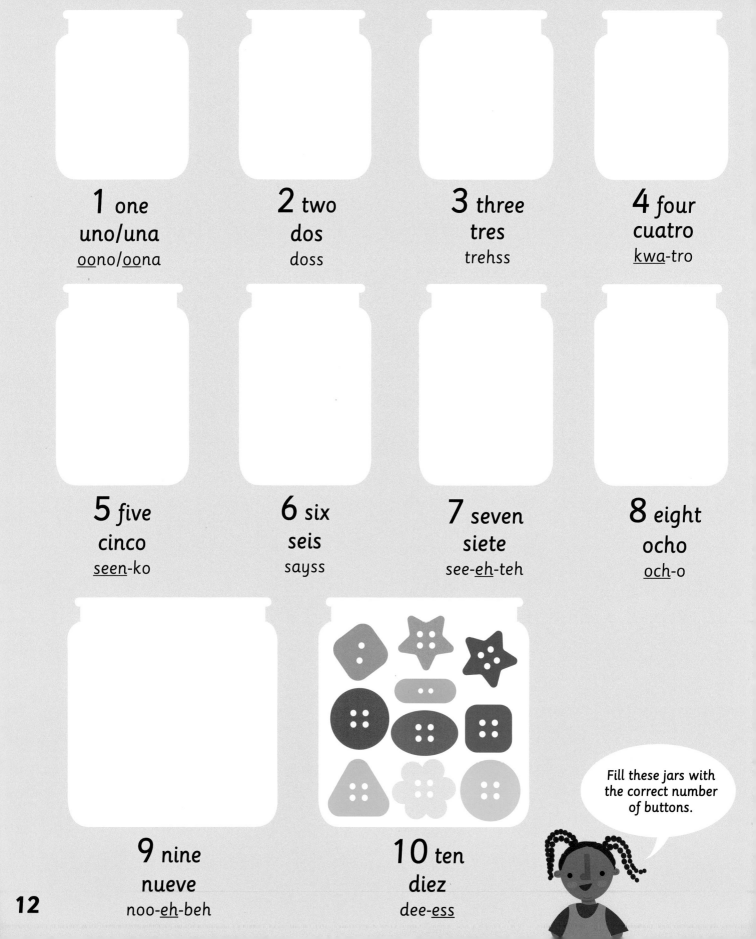

1 one
uno/una
oono/oona

2 two
dos
doss

3 three
tres
trehss

4 four
cuatro
kwa-tro

5 five
cinco
seen-ko

6 six
seis
sayss

7 seven
siete
see-eh-teh

8 eight
ocho
och-o

9 nine
nueve
noo-eh-beh

10 ten
diez
dee-ess

Fill these jars with
the correct number
of buttons.

Colors

green

red

yellow

pink

blue

brown

orange

morado/morada
mor<u>ah</u>-doh/mor<u>ah</u>-da

negro/negra
<u>neh</u>gro/<u>neh</u>gra

blanco/blanca
<u>blan</u>ko/<u>blan</u>ka

Put a "¡bravo!" sticker here when you complete the page.

13

Tu cabeza
too ka<u>beh</u>-sa

Can you name the parts of the head and find the stickers to match?

la cabeza
la ka<u>beh</u>-sa

el mentón
el men-<u>ton</u>

el diente
el dee-<u>yen</u>-teh

el cuello
el <u>kweh</u>-yo

Your head

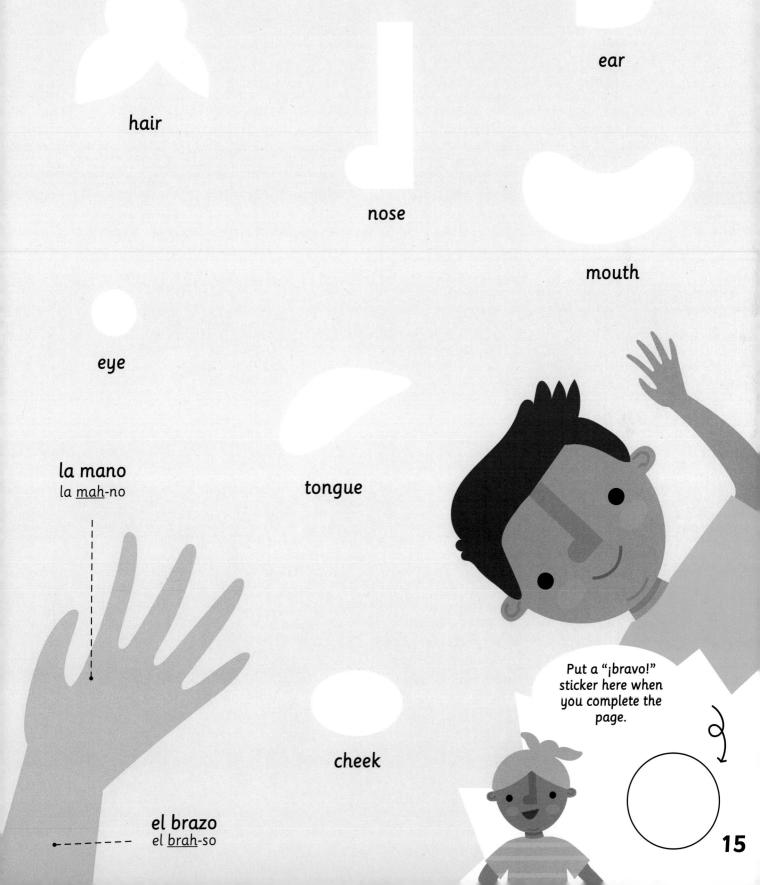

hair

ear

nose

mouth

eye

tongue

la mano
la <u>mah</u>-no

cheek

Put a "¡bravo!" sticker here when you complete the page.

el brazo
el <u>brah</u>-so

La hora del baño

la <u>ora</u> del <u>ban</u>-yo

Bath time

la ducha
la <u>doo</u>cha

el inodoro
el eeh-noh-<u>doh</u>-roh

towel

el lavamanos
el la-bah-<u>mah</u>-noss

soap

shampoo

el patito
el pat-<u>ee</u>-toh

hairbrush

sponge

la bañera
la bany<u>air</u>-a

la pasta de dientes
la <u>pas</u>-ta deh dee-<u>yen</u>-tess

toothbrush

16

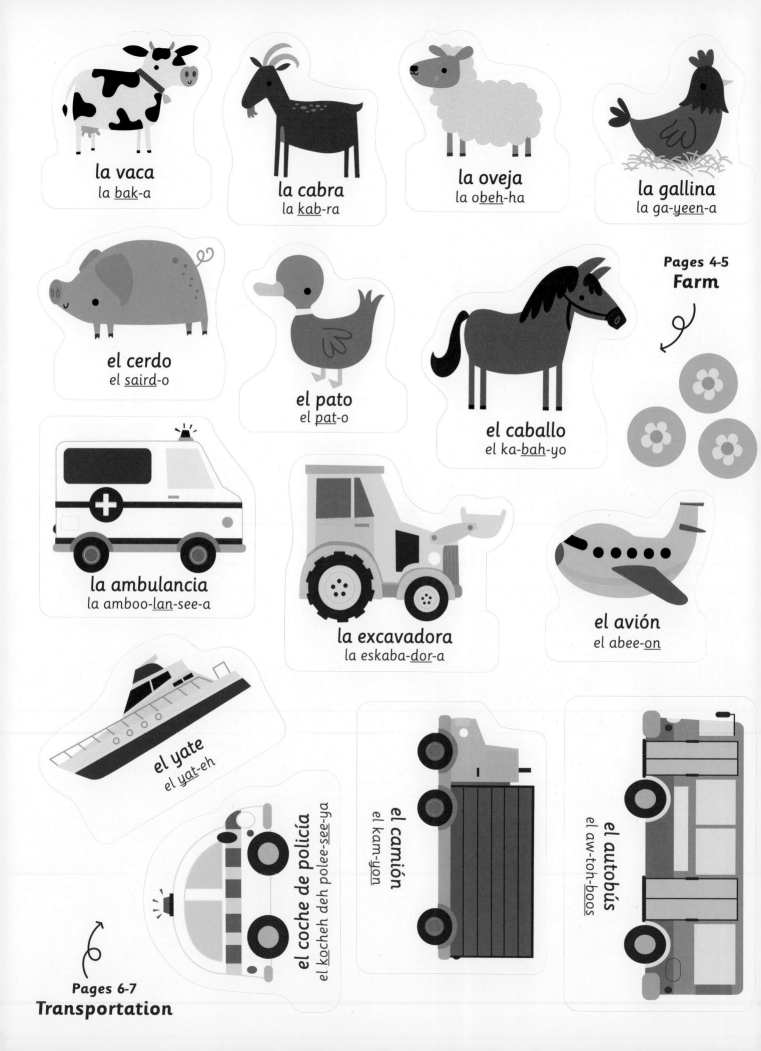

la vaca
la <u>bak</u>-a

la cabra
la <u>kab</u>-ra

la oveja
la <u>obeh</u>-ha

la gallina
la ga-<u>yeen</u>-a

el cerdo
el <u>saird</u>-o

el pato
el <u>pat</u>-o

el caballo
el ka-<u>bah</u>-yo

Pages 4-5
Farm

la ambulancia
la amboo-<u>lan</u>-see-a

la excavadora
la eskaba-<u>dor</u>-a

el avión
el abee-<u>on</u>

el yate
el <u>yat</u>-eh

el coche de policía
el <u>kocheh</u> deh polee-<u>see</u>-ya

el camión
el kam-<u>yon</u>

el autobús
el aw-toh-<u>boos</u>

Pages 6-7
Transportation

el león
el leh-on

el mono
el mon-o

el oso polar
el oh-so pol-lar

el tigre
el tee-greh

la cebra
la seb-ra

la jirafa
la hee-rah-fa

el cubo
el koo-bo

el cocodrilo
el kokko-dree-lo

**Page 12
Numbers**

la concha
la koncha

la gaviota
la gab-yota

el velero
el belair-o

la estrella de mar
la esstreh-ya deh mar

la silla de playa
la see-ya deh plah-ya

el cangrejo
el kangreh-ho

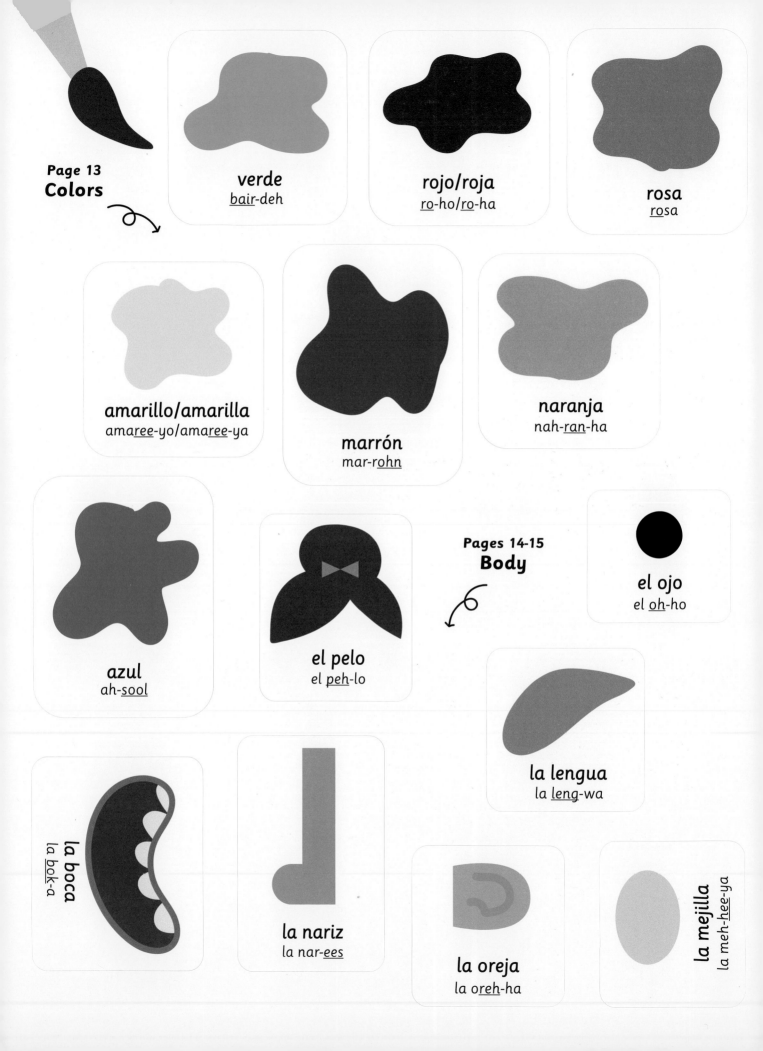

Page 13
Colors

verde
bair-deh

rojo/roja
_ro_-ho/_ro_-ha

rosa
rosa

amarillo/amarilla
ama_ree_-yo/ama_ree_-ya

marrón
mar-_rohn_

naranja
nah-_ran_-ha

azul
ah-_sool_

el pelo
el _peh_-lo

Pages 14-15
Body

el ojo
el _oh_-ho

la lengua
la _leng_-wa

la boca
la _bok_-a

la nariz
la nar-_ees_

la oreja
la o_reh_-ha

la mejilla
la meh-_hee_-ya

el cepillo de dientes
el sep-_ee_-yo deh dee-_yen_-tess

el jabón
el hab_on_

el cepillo del pelo
el sep-_ee_-yo del _peh_-lo

la toalla
la toh-_ah_-ya

la esponja
la ess-_pon_-ha

Page 16
Bath time

el champú
el sham-_poo_

la cuchara
la koo_char_-a

el vaso
el _bah_-so

Page 17
**Setting the
table**

el tenedor
el teneh-_dor_

el tazón
el tas-_on_

el cuchillo
el kooch_ee_-yo

los bloques
loss _blok_-ess

la muñeca
la moon-_yeh_-ka

los lápices de colores
loss _lap_-eesess deh kol-_or_-ess

la pelota
la peh-_lot_-a

el reloj
el rel_okh_

Pages 18-19
**Creative
play**

el osito
el o-_seet_-o

el dinosaurio
el dee-noh-_sahw_-reeo

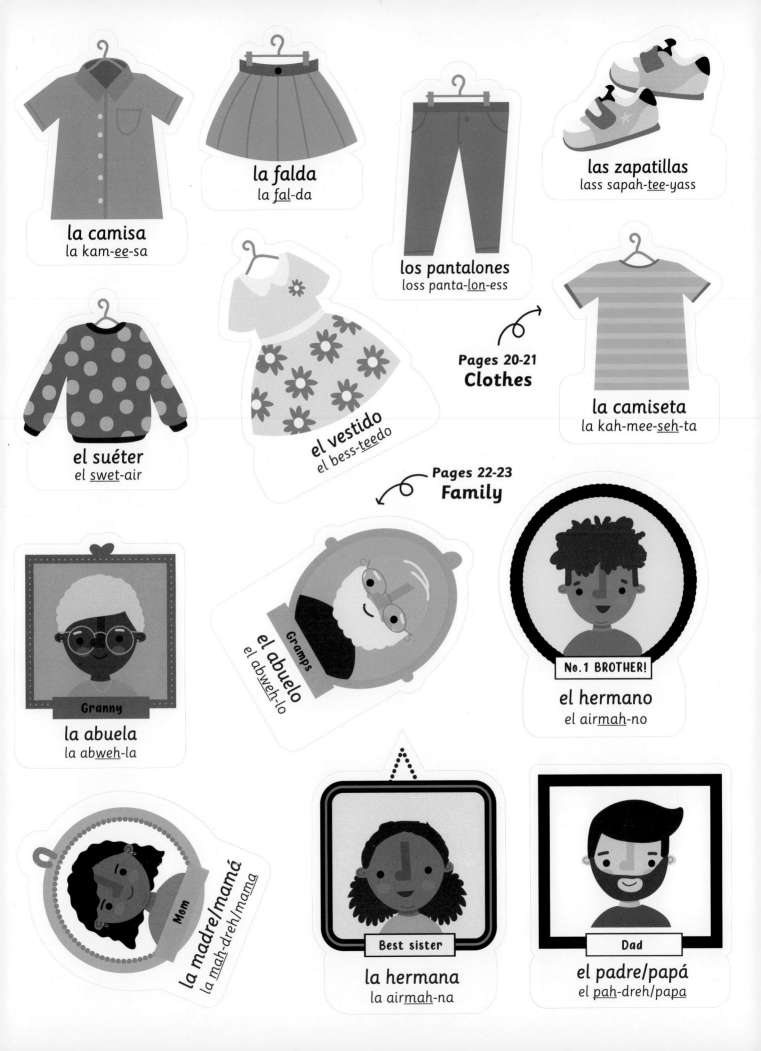

la camisa
la kam-<u>ee</u>-sa

la falda
la <u>fal</u>-da

los pantalones
loss panta-<u>lon</u>-ess

las zapatillas
lass sapah-<u>tee</u>-yass

el suéter
el <u>swet</u>-air

el vestido
el bess-<u>teedo</u>

Pages 20-21
Clothes

la camiseta
la kah-mee-<u>seh</u>-ta

Pages 22-23
Family

Granny
la abuela
la ab<u>weh</u>-la

Gramps
el abuelo
el ab<u>weh</u>-lo

No.1 BROTHER!
el hermano
el air<u>mah</u>-no

Mom
la madre/mamá
la <u>mah</u>-dreh/<u>mama</u>

Best sister
la hermana
la air<u>mah</u>-na

Dad
el padre/papá
el <u>pah</u>-dreh/<u>papa</u>

Page 24
Park

el columpio
el kol-<u>oom</u>-pee-o

el cajón de arena
el ka-<u>hon</u> deh ah-<u>reh</u>na

el tobogán
el tobo-<u>gan</u>

el muñeco de nieve
el moon-<u>yek</u>-o deh nee-<u>eh</u>-beh

el árbol
el <u>ar</u>-bol

la bicicleta
la bee-see-<u>kleh</u>-ta

Page 25
Weather

el sol
el sol

la lluvia
la <u>yoo</u>-beea

las nubes
lass <u>noo</u>-bess

la tormenta
la tor-<u>men</u>-ta

la nieve
la nee-<u>eh</u>-beh

el viento
el bee-<u>en</u>-toh

el arroz
el ahr-<u>rohs</u>

el queso
el <u>keh</u>-so

el azúcar
el ah-<u>soo</u>-kar

la carne
la <u>kar</u>-neh

la mantequilla
la manteh-<u>kee</u>-ya

el huevo
el <u>weh</u>-bo

la leche
la <u>leh</u>-cheh

Pages 26-27
Supermarket

los arándanos
loss ah-<u>ran</u>-dan-oss

las naranjas
lass nah-<u>ran</u>-hass

la sandía
la san-<u>dee</u>-ya

los pimientos
loss pee-<u>myen</u>-toss

los plátanos
los <u>plah</u>-tan-oss

el maíz
el mah-<u>ees</u>

los guisantes
loss gui-<u>sahn</u>-tess

Pages 28-29
**Market
stall**

los melocotones
loss melo-ko-<u>ton</u>-ess

la col
la kol

las papas
lass <u>pah</u>-pass

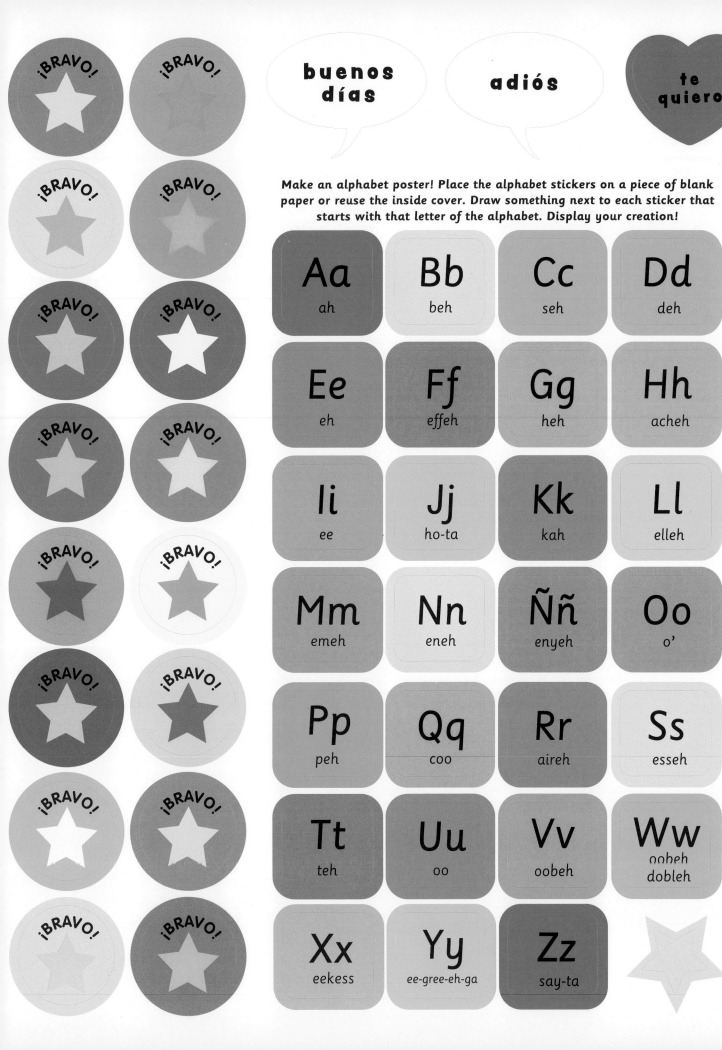

buenos días

adiós

te quiero

Make an alphabet poster! Place the alphabet stickers on a piece of blank paper or reuse the inside cover. Draw something next to each sticker that starts with that letter of the alphabet. Display your creation!

Aa ah	Bb beh	Cc seh	Dd deh
Ee eh	Ff effeh	Gg heh	Hh acheh
Ii ee	Jj ho-ta	Kk kah	Ll elleh
Mm emeh	Nn eneh	Ññ enyeh	Oo o'
Pp peh	Qq coo	Rr aireh	Ss esseh
Tt teh	Uu oo	Vv oobeh	Ww oobeh dobleh
Xx eekess	Yy ee-gree-eh-ga	Zz say-ta	

Poniendo la mesa

pon-<u>yen</u>do la <u>meh</u>-ssa

Setting the table

bowl

la jarra
la <u>hah</u>-ra

glass

spoon

el plato
el <u>plah</u>-toh

fork

knife

Put a "¡bravo!" sticker here when you complete the page.

17

El juego creativo
el <u>hweh</u>-go kreh-ah-<u>tee</u>-bo

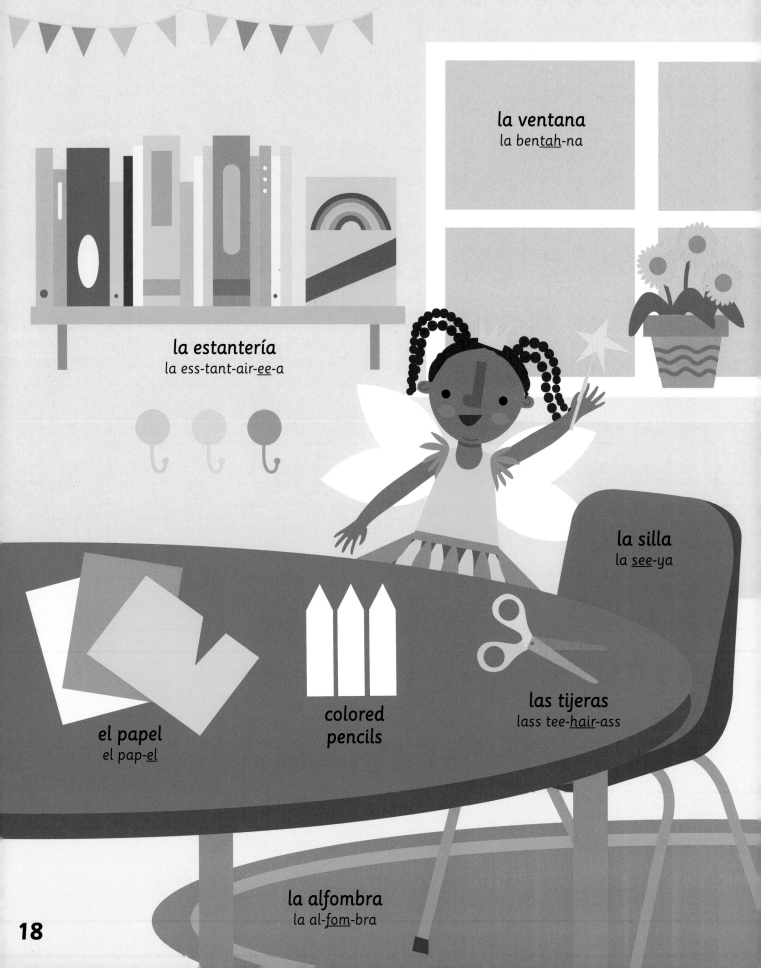

la ventana
la ben<u>tah</u>-na

la estantería
la ess-tant-air-<u>ee</u>-a

la silla
la <u>see</u>-ya

el papel
el pap-<u>el</u>

colored
pencils

las tijeras
lass tee-<u>hair</u>-ass

la alfombra
la al-<u>fom</u>-bra

Creative play

clock

teddy bear

doll

el cuadro
el <u>kwa</u>-dro

ball

blocks

dinosaur

Put a "¡bravo!" sticker here when you complete the page.

19

La ropa
la <u>ro</u>-pa

las botas
lass <u>boh</u>-tass

los zapatos
loss zapah-toss

la gorra
la <u>gor</u>-rah

el abrigo
el ab<u>ree</u>-go

el pijama
el pee<u>hah</u>-ma

los calcetines
loss kalseh-<u>tee</u>-ness

Clothes

skirt

dress

sweater

shirt

pants

el cárdigan
el kar-dee-gan

T-shirt

los pantalones cortos
loss panta-lon-ess kor-toss

sneakers

Put a "¡bravo!" sticker here when you complete the page.

21

La familia
la fam-<u>eel</u>-ya

grandfather

PATCH THE CAT

grandmother

brother

UNCLE DAN

el tío
el <u>tee</u>-yo

AUNT ALEX

MY OLDEST GRANDSON

SCOUT THE DOG

la tía
la <u>tee</u>-ya

el nieto
el <u>nee</u>-<u>eh</u>-toh

Family

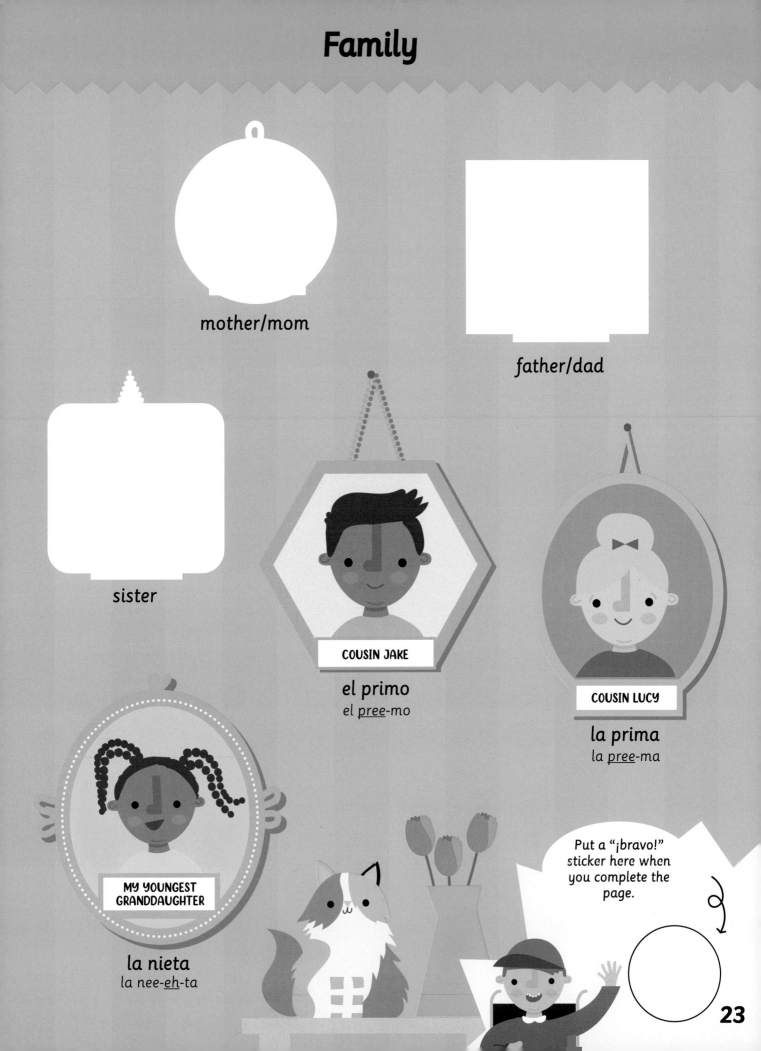

mother/mom

father/dad

sister

COUSIN JAKE

el primo
el <u>pree</u>-mo

COUSIN LUCY

la prima
la <u>pree</u>-ma

MY YOUNGEST
GRANDDAUGHTER

la nieta
la nee-<u>eh</u>-ta

Put a "¡bravo!"
sticker here when
you complete the
page.

El tiempo

el tee-<u>em</u>po

Weather

sunshine

clouds

storm

snow

snowman

rain

wind

el arco iris

el arko <u>eer</u>-iss

Put a "¡bravo!" sticker here when you complete the page.

El supermercado
el soopair-mair-<u>kah</u>-doh

rice

milk

el pescado
el pes<u>kah</u>-do

la bolsa de la compra
la <u>bol</u>sa deh la <u>kom</u>pra

Can you find all the stickers?

Supermarket

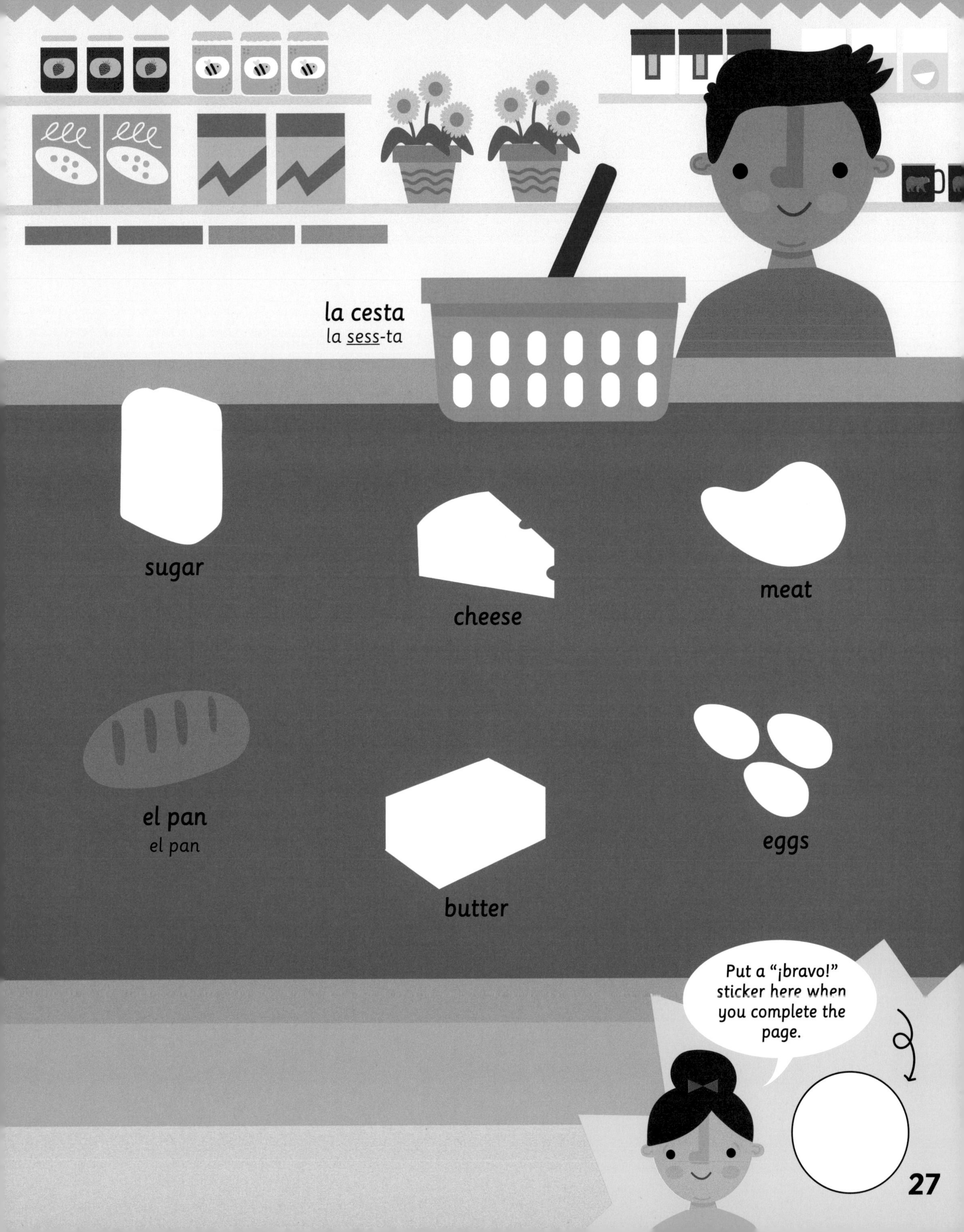

la cesta
la <u>sess</u>-ta

sugar

cheese

meat

el pan
el pan

butter

eggs

Put a "¡bravo!" sticker here when you complete the page.

El puesto del mercado
el pwehs-toh del mair-kah-do

la piña
la peen-ya

bananas

las manzanas
lass man-sah-nass

oranges

peaches

las uvas
lass oobass

los limones
loss leemon-ess

watermelon

What is your favorite fruit or vegetable?

la fresa
la freh-sa

blueberries

las frambuesas
lass fram-bweh-sass

28

Market stall

los tomates
loss tom-_ah_-tess

potatoes

cabbage

corn

el brócoli
el _brok_-olee

peppers

las zanahorias
lass sanah-_or_-ee-ass

peas

Put a "¡bravo!" sticker here when you complete the page.

Word list - Lista de palabras

leess-ta deh pa-lab-rass

Español/Spanish – Inglés/English

el abrigo coat
abril April
la abuela grandmother
el abuelo grandfather
agosto August
la alfombra rug
amarillo/amarilla yellow
la ambulancia ambulance
los arándanos blueberries
el árbol tree
el arco iris rainbow
la arena sand
el arroz rice
el autobús bus
el avión airplane
el azúcar sugar
azul blue
el plátano bananas
la bañera bathtub
la bicicleta bicycle
blanco/blanca white
los bloques blocks
la boca mouth
la bolsa de la compra shopping bag
las botas boots
el brazo arm
el brócoli broccoli
el caballo horse
la cabeza head
la cabra goat
el cajón de arena sandbox
los calcetines socks
el camión truck
el camión de bomberos fire engine
la camisa shirt
la camiseta T-shirt
el cangrejo crab
el cárdigan cardigan
la carne meat
el castillo de arena sandcastle
la cebra zebra
el cepillo de dientes toothbrush
el cepillo del pelo brush
el cerdo pig
la cesta basket
el champú shampoo
cinco five

el coche car
el coche de policía police car
el cocodrilo crocodile
la col cabbage
los colores colors
el columpio swing
la concha shell
el cuadro painting
cuatro four
el cubo pail
la cuchara spoon
el cuchillo knife
el cuello neck
el día day
diciembre December
el diente tooth
diez ten
el dinosaurio dinosaur
domingo Sunday
dos two
la ducha shower
el elefante elephant
enero January
la esponja sponge
el estanque pond
la estantería bookshelf
la estrella de mar starfish
la excavadora digger
la falda skirt
la familia family
febrero February
el fin de semana weekend
los flores flowers
las frambuesas raspberries
la fresa strawberry
la gallina hen
el gallo rooster
el gato cat
la gaviota seagull
la gorra cap
gracias thank you
la granja farm
los guisantes peas
el helicóptero helicopter
la hermana sister
el hermano brother
el hipopótamo hippopotamus
el huevo eggs
el inodoro toilet

el invierno winter
el jabón soap
la jarra pitcher
la jirafa giraffe
jueves Thursday
julio July
junio June
la derecha right
la izquierda left
los lápices de colores colored pencils
el lavamanos sink
la leche milk
la lengua tongue
el léon lion
los limones lemons
la lluvia rain
lunes Monday
la madre mother
el maíz corn
la mamá mom
la mano hand
la mantequilla butter
las manzanas apples
el mar sea
marrón brown
martes Tuesday
marzo March
mayo May
la mejilla cheek
los melocotones peaches
el mentón chin
la mesa table
miércoles Wednesday
el mono monkey
morado/morada purple
la muñeca doll
el muñeco de nieve snowman
naranja orange
las naranjas oranges
la nariz nose
negro/negra black
la nieta granddaughter
el nieto grandson
la nieve snow
no no
la noche night
noviembre November
las nubes clouds
nueve nine

los **números** numbers
ocho eight
octubre October
el **ojo** eye
la **oreja** ear
el **osito** teddy bear
el **oso polar** polar bear
el **otoño** fall
la **oveja** sheep
el **padre** father
el **pan** bread
los **pantalones** pants
los **pantalones cortos** shorts
el **papá** dad
las **papas** potatoes
el **papel** paper
el **parque** park
la **pasta de dientes** toothpaste
el **patito** rubber duck
el **pato** duck
el **pelo** hair
la **pelota** ball
el **perro** dog
el **pescado** fish
el **pijama** pajamas
los **pimientos** peppers
la **piña** pineapple
el **plato** plate
la **playa** beach
por favor please
la **prima** cousin (female)
la **primavera** spring
el **primo** cousin (male)
el **puesto** market stall
el **queso** cheese
el **reloj** clock
rojo/roja red
la **ropa** clothes
rosa pink
sábado Saturday
la **sandía** watermelon
seis six
septiembre September
sí yes
siete seven
la **silla** chair
la **silla de playa** beach chair
el **sol** sunshine
la **sombrilla** beach umbrella
el **suéter** sweater
el **supermercado** supermarket
la **surfista** surfer (female)
el **surfista** surfer (male)
el **tazón** bowl

el **tenedor** fork
la **tía** aunt
el **tiempo** weather
el **tigre** tiger
las **tijeras** scissors
el **tío** uncle
la **toalla** towel
el **tobogán** slide
los **tomates** tomatoes
la **tormenta** storm
el **tren** train
tres three
uno/una one
las **uvas** grapes
la **vaca** cow
el **vaso** glass
el **velero** sailboat
la **ventana** window
el **verano** summer
verde green
el **vestido** dress
el **viento** wind
viernes Friday
el **yate** yacht
las **zanahorias** carrots
las **zapatillas** sneakers
los **zapatos** shoes
el **zoológico** zoo

English/Inglés – Spanish/Español

airplane el avión
ambulance la ambulancia
apples las manzanas
April abril
arm el brazo
August agosto
aunt la tía
ball la pelota
bananas el plátano
basket la cesta
bathtub la bañera
beach la playa
beach chair la silla de playa
beach umbrella la sombrilla
bicycle la bicicleta
black negro/negra
blocks los bloques
blue azul
blueberries los arándanos
bookshelf la estantería
boots las botas
bowl el tazón
bread el pan

broccoli el brócoli
brother el hermano
brown marrón
brush el cepillo del pelo
bus el autobús
butter la mantequilla
cabbage la col
cap la gorra
car el coche
cardigan el cárdigan
carrots las zanahorias
cat el gato
chair la silla
cheek la mejilla
cheese el queso
chin el mentón
clock el reloj
clothes la ropa
clouds las nubes
coat el abrigo
colored pencils los lápices de colores
colors los colores
corn el maíz
cousin (female) la prima
cousin (male) el primo
cow la vaca
crab el cangrejo
crocodile el cocodrilo
dad el papá
day el día
December diciembre
digger la excavadora
dinosaur el dinosaurio
dog el perro
doll la muñeca
dress el vestido
duck el pato
ear la oreja
eggs el huevo
eight ocho
elephant el elefante
eye el ojo
fall el otoño
family la familia
farm la granja
father el padre
February febrero
fish el pescado
fire engine el camión de bomberos
five cinco
flowers los flores
fork el tenedor
four cuatro
Friday viernes

31

giraffe la jirafa
glass el vaso
goat la cabra
granddaughter la nieta
grandfather el abuelo
grandmother la abuela
grandson el nieto
grapes las uvas
green verde
hair el pelo
hand la mano
head la cabeza
helicopter el helicóptero
hen la gallina
hippopotamus el hipopótamo
horse el caballo
January enero
July julio
June junio
knife el cuchillo
left la izquierda
lemons los limones
lion el léon
March marzo
market stall el puesto
May mayo
meat la carne
milk la leche
mom la mamá
Monday lunes
monkey el mono
mother la madre
mouth la boca
neck el cuello
night la noche
nine nueve
no no
nose la nariz
November noviembre
numbers los números
October octubre
one uno/una
orange naranja
oranges las naranjas
pail el cubo
painting el cuadro
pajamas el pijama
pants los pantalones
paper el papel
park el parque
peaches los melocotones
peas los guisantes
peppers los pimientos
pig el cerdo

pineapple la piña
pink rosa
pitcher la jarra
plate el plato
please por favor
polar bear el oso polar
police car el coche de policía
pond el estanque
potatoes las papas
purple morado/morada
rain la lluvia
rainbow el arco iris
raspberries las frambuesas
red rojo/roja
rice el arroz
right la derecha
rooster el gallo
rubber duck el patito
rug la alfombra
sailboat el velero
sand la arena
sandbox el cajón de arena
sandcastle el castillo de arena
Saturday sábado
scissors las tijeras
sea el mar
seagull la gaviota
September septiembre
seven siete
shampoo el champú
sheep la oveja
shell la concha
shirt la camisa
shoes los zapatos
shopping bag la bolsa de la compra
shorts los pantalones cortos
shower la ducha
sink el lavamanos
sister la hermana
six seis
skirt la falda
slide el tobogán
sneakers las zapatillas
snow la nieve
snowman el muñeco de nieve
soap el jabón
socks los calcetines
sponge la esponja
spoon la cuchara
spring la primavera
starfish la estrella de mar
storm la tormenta
strawberry la fresa
sugar el azúcar

summer el verano
Sunday domingo
sunshine el sol
supermarket el supermercado
surfer (female) la surfista
surfer (male) el surfista
sweater el suéter
swing el columpio
T-shirt la camiseta
table la mesa
teddy bear el osito
ten diez
thank you gracias
three tres
Thursday jueves
tiger el tigre
toilet el inodoro
tomatoes los tomates
tongue la lengua
tooth el diente
toothbrush el cepillo de dientes
toothpaste la pasta de dientes
towel la toalla
train el tren
tree el árbol
truck el camión
Tuesday martes
two dos
uncle el tío
watermelon la sandía
weather el tiempo
Wednesday miércoles
weekend el fin de semana
white blanco/blanca
wind el viento
window la ventana
winter el invierno
yacht el yate
yellow amarillo/amarilla
yes sí
zebra la cebra
zoo el zoológico

goodbye
adiós
ah-dee<u>yoss</u>

32